Finding Shelter in the Storm

a 5-minute gratitude journal of reflection for Christian women dealing with a narcissist

Copyright © 2022 Trillium Sage Publishing

All rights reserved. This book or any portion thereof may not be reproduced or used in any manner whatsoever without the express written permission of the publisher except for the use of brief quotations in a book review.

ISBN: 978-1-958118-06-1

Trillium Sage Publishing
3943 Irvine Blvd #138, Irvine, CA 92602
www.TrilliumSage.com

Scripture quotations are from the ESV® Bible (The Holy Bible, English Standard Version®), copyright © 2001 by Crossway, a publishing ministry of Good News Publishers. Used by permission. All rights reserved. The ESV text may not be quoted in any publication made available to the public by a Creative Commons license. The ESV may not be translated into any other language.

A Free Gift for You

Did you just discover the difficult relationship in your life is with a narcissist? I polled thousands of survivors and asked one simple question:

What were the most impactful first steps you took in your narcissistic abuse recovery?

This is what they told me.
Download your free guide below!

YOUR 7 STEP JOURNEY TO NARCISSISTIC ABUSE RECOVERY

GRAB YOUR FREE GUIDE AT TRILLIUMSAGE.COM

INCLUDES:
- THE KEY 7 STRATEGIES TO KICKSTART YOUR HEALING
- THE CRITICAL FIRST STEP THAT HAS HAD THE MOST IMPACT FOR SURVIVORS
- HOW TO CREATE THE IDEAL SUPPORT SYSTEM FOR YOUR JOURNEY

Also from Trillium Sage Publishing

"...book reminds me I am not alone and there is help..."

"...I wish this book could have been available years ago as I had to navigate the waters of abuse and abandonment."

"...informative, compassionate, and insightful read."

Available on Amazon and Audible

Launching Summer 2022

This journal belongs to:

To get the most out of this journal

For any Christian who has experienced narcissistic abuse, you undoubtedly find yourself asking, "Where is God in my madness?!" It is paramount that during these trials, we cling to Him more than ever. This journal aims to help you in these challenging times by improving your mental health as you begin to rebuild and regain your sense of self.

As you may already be aware, journaling is a powerful way to improve your mental health (Brennan, 2021). Some quick ways journaling can help:
- decreases anxiety
- creates awareness
- regulates emotions
- quickens physical healing

Journaling doesn't have to be long, drawn out, or tedious. It's not to be something for you to dread. There may be days when you just don't want to get out of bed. There may also be days where taking a shower is all you can muster. My hope is that as you trudge through the muck, you will be able to find just five minutes every day to consider:
- three things that you are grateful for
- one main goal for the day
- one thing that you'll do that day to find joy
- a time of reflection

Gratitude

Having a spirit of gratitude helps your mental health tremendously (Morin, 2015). Not only does being aware of all that you have to be thankful for help in improving your psychological health, but it also helps with improving self-esteem and quality of sleep - fortifying your mental strength. There is nothing too big or too small to appreciate! Need some ideas? Here are some areas to consider being thankful:
- loving family
- Fridays
- technology
- pets

- a cozy bed
- good health
- rainbows
- air conditioning
- your senses
- clean water
- hugs
- naptime
- the sun's warmth
- best friends
- teachers
- music
- fresh air
- ice cream
- relaxing baths
- comfort food

What's your ONE thing?

Years ago, I read *The ONE Thing* by Gary Keller and Jay Papasan. This book showed the power in prioritizing the most important action that will move the needle. For this journal, I'd like for you to think of just ONE thing that you need to get done for the day. It can be a trivial matter or something more, but it is the one goal you would like to accomplish for the day. Writing it down in your **Daily Check-In** will make your day more intentional and when you end your day having completed your one thing, you will have an awesome sense of accomplishment. Remember, your one thing can be the simplest task. Stay focused on that *one* thing and hit your goal!

Find joy

I'm a big believer in self-care. Part of self-care is ensuring that you give yourself opportunities to find joy in your daily living. Be intentional about this! Years ago a therapist shared with me that we should carve out an hour a day to just do something for ourselves. Depending on what brings you joy, it could be at the beginning of the day, at the end of the day, or anytime in between. For me, sometimes it could be just cozying up in bed and ending the day watching an old re-run of my favorite sitcom. Where you do find joy? Hopefully this list will spur some ideas for you:

- going for a walk in nature
- painting
- shopping
- taking the dog on a trip
- chatting with a friend
- reading the Bible
- enjoying a hot cup of coffee
- exercising even for a short while

- getting a facial
- trying out a new wine
- making cookies
- planning a trip
- writing a letter
- helping out a neighbor
- surprising the kids with a treat
- decluttering a room
- watching a show
- telling someone I love them
- taking a bath
- re-organizing a space

A Time for Reflection

This part of your daily journaling can be as much or as little as you would like to make it. Full sentences, bullet points...whatever floats your boat. Can't think of what to write? Maybe just copying the verse of the day will help. You can jot down a quick prayer or praise, write what that day's Scripture means to you, or if necessary, bring your pain to God. Feel free to write whatever is on your mind. Getting it from your brain to your hand and eventually to paper will help to release any thoughts that you have been holding onto.

I hope that you will find this journal helpful as you weather the storm you are in. You may currently be in the midst of despair, but be proactive in how you get through it. Be thankful, set goals, do your best to find joy. You are never alone: God sees everything that you're experiencing. Days, weeks, and months from now, when you go back and flip through your journal entries, my hope is that you might realize just how far you've come!

Looking for Support?

If you are interested in joining an online support group, I encourage you to visit us at : https://www.facebook.com/groups/christiansupportfornarcissisticabuserecovery

You may scan the QR code to be taken there directly:

Hope to see you soon!

All Scripture is breathed out by God and profitable for teaching, for reproof, for correction, and for training in righteousness, that the man of God may be complete, equipped for every good work.

2 Timothy 3:16-17

Daily check-in

date: _____

today I am thankful for:

1. _____

2. _____

3. _____

my ONE goal today:

today I will find joy in:

reflection:

May the God of hope fill you with all joy and peace as you trust in him, so that you may overflow with hope by the power of the Holy Spirit.
Romans 15:13

Daily check-in

date:

today I am thankful for:

1.

2.

3.

my ONE goal today:

today I will find joy in:

reflection:

For I know the plans I have for you, declares the Lord, plans for welfare and not for evil, to give you a future and a hope.
Jeremiah 29:11

Daily check-in

date:

today I am thankful for:

1.
2.
3.

my ONE goal today:

today I will find joy in:

reflection:

...do not be anxious about anything, but in everything by prayer and supplication with thanksgiving let your requests be made known to God.
Philippians 4:6

Daily check-in

date: _____

today I am thankful for:

1. _____
2. _____
3. _____

my ONE goal today:

_____

today I will find joy in:

_____

reflection:

_____
_____
_____
_____
_____
_____
_____
_____

...I am with you always, to the end of the age.
Matthew 28:20

Daily check-in

date:

today I am thankful for:

1.
2.
3.

my ONE goal today:

today I will find joy in:

reflection:

You are a hiding place for me;
you preserve me from trouble;
you surround me with shouts of deliverance.
Psalm 32:7

Daily check-in

date:

today I am thankful for:

1.

2.

3.

my ONE goal today:

today I will find joy in:

reflection:

But Jesus looked at them and said,
"With man this is impossible, but with God all things are possible."
Matthew 19:26

Daily check-in

date:

today I am thankful for:

1.
2.
3.

my ONE goal today:

today I will find joy in:

reflection:

> For I, the Lord your God, hold your right hand;
> it is I who say to you,
> "Fear not, I am the one who helps you."
> Isaiah 41:13

Daily check-in

date:

today I am thankful for:

1.
2.
3.

my ONE goal today:

today I will find joy in:

reflection:

*A joyful heart is good medicine,
but a crushed spirit dries up the bones.
Proverbs 17:22*

Daily check-in

date:

today I am thankful for:

1.
2.
3.

my ONE goal today:

today I will find joy in:

reflection:

...The Lord will fight for you, and you have only to be silent.
Exodus 14:14

Daily check-in

date: _____

today I am thankful for:

1. _____

2. _____

3. _____

my ONE goal today:

_____

today I will find joy in:

_____

reflection:

_____

_____

_____

_____

_____

_____

_____

_____

If any of you lacks wisdom, let him ask God, who gives generously to all without reproach, and it will be given him.

James 1:5

Daily check-in

date:

today I am thankful for:

1.
2.
3.

my ONE goal today:

today I will find joy in:

reflection:

*The Lord your God is in your midst, a mighty one who will save;
he will rejoice over you with gladness; he will quiet you by his love;
he will exult over you with loud singing.*
Zephaniah 3:17

Daily check-in

date: _____

today I am thankful for:

1. _____
2. _____
3. _____

my ONE goal today:

_____

today I will find joy in:

_____

reflection:

_____
_____
_____
_____
_____
_____
_____
_____

No temptation has overtaken you that is not common to man. God is faithful, and he will not let you be tempted beyond your ability, but with the temptation he will also provide the way of escape, that you may be able to endure it.

1 Corinthians 10:13

Daily check-in

date:

today I am thankful for:

1.

2.

3.

my ONE goal today:

today I will find joy in:

reflection:

*He is not afraid of bad news;
his heart is firm, trusting in the Lord.
Psalm 112:7*

Daily check-in

date:

today I am thankful for:

1.

2.

3.

my ONE goal today:

today I will find joy in:

reflection:

*God is our refuge and strength,
a very present help in trouble.
Psalm 46:1*

Daily check-in

date:

today I am thankful for:

1.
2.
3.

my ONE goal today:

today I will find joy in:

reflection:

Now faith is the assurance of things hoped for, the conviction of things not seen.
Hebrews 11:1

Daily check-in

date:

today I am thankful for:

1.

2.

3.

my ONE goal today:

today I will find joy in:

reflection:

...for they all saw him and were terrified. But immediately he spoke to them and said, "Take heart; it is I. Do not be afraid."

Mark 6:50

Daily check-in

date:

today I am thankful for:

1.
2.
3.

my ONE goal today:

today I will find joy in:

reflection:

*You keep him in perfect peace whose mind is stayed on you,
because he trusts in you.
Isaiah 26:3*

Daily check-in

date:

today I am thankful for:

1.

2.

3.

my ONE goal today:

today I will find joy in:

reflection:

And he said to his disciples,
"Therefore I tell you, do not be anxious about your life, what you will eat,
nor about your body, what you will put on...
Luke 12:22

Daily check-in

date: _____

today I am thankful for:

1. _____

2. _____

3. _____

my ONE goal today:

_____

today I will find joy in:

_____

reflection:

_____

_____

_____

_____

_____

_____

_____

_____

The Lord will fulfill his purpose for me;
your steadfast love, O Lord, endures forever.
Do not forsake the work of your hands.
Psalm 138:8

Daily check-in

date:

today I am thankful for:

1.
2.
3.

my ONE goal today:

today I will find joy in:

reflection:

And we know that for those who love God all things work together for good, for those who are called according to his purpose.

Romans 8:28

Daily check-in

date:

today I am thankful for:

1.

2.

3.

my ONE goal today:

today I will find joy in:

reflection:

May the God of hope fill you with all joy and peace in believing, so that by the power of the Holy Spirit you may abound in hope.
Romans 15:13

Daily check-in

date:

today I am thankful for:

1.
2.
3.

my ONE goal today:

today I will find joy in:

reflection:

*The name of the Lord is a strong tower;
the righteous man runs into it and is safe.*
Proverbs 18:10

Daily check-in

date:

today I am thankful for:

1.

2.

3.

my ONE goal today:

today I will find joy in:

reflection:

...for God gave us a spirit not of fear but of power and love and self-control.
2 Timothy 1:7

Daily check-in

date:

today I am thankful for:

1.
2.
3.

my ONE goal today:

today I will find joy in:

reflection:

There is no fear in love, but perfect love casts out fear. For fear has to do with punishment, and whoever fears has not been perfected in love.
1 John 4:18

Daily check-in

date:

today I am thankful for:

1.
2.
3.

my ONE goal today:

today I will find joy in:

reflection:

...He will wipe away every tear from their eyes, and death shall be no more, neither shall there be mourning, nor crying, nor pain anymore, for the former things have passed away.
Revelation 21:4

Daily check-in

date:

today I am thankful for:

1.

2.

3.

my ONE goal today:

today I will find joy in:

reflection:

Therefore, my beloved brothers, be steadfast, immovable, always abounding in the work of the Lord, knowing that in the Lord your labor is not in vain.
1 Corinthians 15:58

Daily check-in

date:

today I am thankful for:

1.
2.
3.

my ONE goal today:

today I will find joy in:

reflection:

And which of you by being anxious can add a single hour to his span of life?
Luke 12:25

Daily check-in

date:

today I am thankful for:

1.
2.
3.

my ONE goal today:

today I will find joy in:

reflection:

*"Be still, and know that I am God.
I will be exalted among the nations,
I will be exalted in the earth!"*
Psalm 46:10

Daily check-in

date:

today I am thankful for:

1.
2.
3.

my ONE goal today:

today I will find joy in:

reflection:

...Have I not commanded you? Be strong and courageous. Do not be frightened, and do not be dismayed, for the Lord your God is with you wherever you go."
Joshua 1:9

Daily check-in

date:

today I am thankful for:

1.

2.

3.

my ONE goal today:

today I will find joy in:

reflection:

*Be still before the Lord and wait patiently for him;
fret not yourself over the one who prospers in his way,
over the man who carries out evil devices!
Psalm 37:7*

Daily check-in

date:

today I am thankful for:

1.

2.

3.

my ONE goal today:

today I will find joy in:

reflection:

*But seek first the kingdom of God and his righteousness,
and all these things will be added to you.
Matthew 6:33*

Monthly check-in

How are you feeling right now, in this moment?

| Depressed | Sad | Neutral | Happy | Joyful |

Name 5 dominant emotions this past month:

_____

_____

_____

_____

_____

What do you feel good about?

_____

_____

_____

What are some things that trigger negative emotions?

_____

_____

_____

What is ONE thing you can do to improve your mental health next month?

_____

..For the battle is the Lord's, and
he will give you into our hand.

1 Samuel 17:47

Daily check-in

date:

today I am thankful for:

1.

2.

3.

my ONE goal today:

today I will find joy in:

reflection:

*What then shall we say to these things?
If God is for us, who can be against us?
Romans 8:31*

Daily check-in

date:

today I am thankful for:

1.

2.

3.

my ONE goal today:

today I will find joy in:

reflection:

When I am afraid, I put my trust in you.
Psalm 56:3

Daily check-in

date:

today I am thankful for:

1.

2.

3.

my ONE goal today:

today I will find joy in:

reflection:

*And my God will supply every need of yours
according to his riches in glory in Christ Jesus.
Philippians 4:19*

Daily check-in

date: _____

today I am thankful for:

1. _____
2. _____
3. _____

my ONE goal today:

_____

today I will find joy in:

_____

reflection:

_____
_____
_____
_____
_____
_____
_____
_____

*But overhearing what they said, Jesus said to the ruler of the synagogue,
"Do not fear, only believe."
Mark 5:36*

Daily check-in

date:

today I am thankful for:

1.
2.
3.

my ONE goal today:

today I will find joy in:

reflection:

*May the God of hope fill you with all joy and peace in believing,
so that by the power of the Holy Spirit you may abound in hope.
Romans 15:13*

Daily check-in

date: _____

today I am thankful for:

1. _____

2. _____

3. _____

my ONE goal today:

_____

today I will find joy in:

_____

reflection:

_____
_____
_____
_____
_____
_____
_____
_____

Peace I leave with you; my peace I give to you. Not as the world gives do I give to you. Let not your hearts be troubled, neither let them be afraid.
John 14:27

Daily check-in

date: _____

today I am thankful for:

1. _____
2. _____
3. _____

my ONE goal today:

_____

today I will find joy in:

_____

reflection:

_____
_____
_____
_____
_____
_____
_____
_____

And let the peace of Christ rule in your hearts,
to which indeed you were called in one body.
And be thankful.
Colossians 3:15

# Daily check-in

date:

today I am thankful for:

1.
2.
3.

my ONE goal today:

today I will find joy in:

reflection:

You shall not fear them, for it is the Lord your God who fights for you.
Deuteronomy 3:22

Daily check-in

date:

today I am thankful for:

1.

2.

3.

my ONE goal today:

today I will find joy in:

reflection:

Keep your life free from love of money, and be content with what you have, for he has said, "I will never leave you nor forsake you."

Hebrews 13:5

Daily check-in

date:

today I am thankful for:

1.

2.

3.

my ONE goal today:

today I will find joy in:

reflection:

> ...but they who wait for the Lord shall renew their strength;
> they shall mount up with wings like eagles;
> they shall run and not be weary;
> they shall walk and not faint.
> Isaiah 40:31

Daily check-in

date: _____

today I am thankful for:

1. _____
2. _____
3. _____

my ONE goal today:

_____

today I will find joy in:

_____

reflection:

_____
_____
_____
_____
_____
_____
_____
_____
_____

*And he awoke and rebuked the wind and said to the sea, "Peace! Be still!"
And the wind ceased, and there was a great calm.
He said to them, "Why are you so afraid? Have you still no faith?"
Mark 4:39-40*

Daily check-in

date:

today I am thankful for:

1.
2.
3.

my ONE goal today:

today I will find joy in:

reflection:

*Therefore do not be anxious, saying,
'What shall we eat?' or 'What shall we drink?' or 'What shall we wear?'
For the Gentiles seek after all these things, and
your heavenly Father knows that you need them all.
Matthew 6:31-32*

Daily check-in

date: _____

today I am thankful for:

1. _____

2. _____

3. _____

my ONE goal today:

_____

today I will find joy in:

_____

reflection:

_____
_____
_____
_____
_____
_____
_____
_____
_____

Brothers, I do not consider that I have made it my own.
But one thing I do:
forgetting what lies behind and straining forward to what lies ahead…
Philippians 3:13

Daily check-in

date:

today I am thankful for:

1.

2.

3.

my ONE goal today:

today I will find joy in:

reflection:

*Trust in the Lord with all your heart,
and do not lean on your own understanding.*
Proverbs 3:5

Daily check-in

date: _____

today I am thankful for:

1. _____
2. _____
3. _____

my ONE goal today:

_____

today I will find joy in:

_____

reflection:

_____
_____
_____
_____
_____
_____
_____
_____

Turn away from evil and do good;
seek peace and pursue it.
Psalm 34:14

Daily check-in

date:

today I am thankful for:

1.

2.

3.

my ONE goal today:

today I will find joy in:

reflection:

When I saw him, I fell at his feet as though dead. But he laid his right hand on me, saying, "Fear not, I am the first and the last...
Revelation 1:17

Daily check-in

date:

today I am thankful for:

1.
2.
3.

my ONE goal today:

today I will find joy in:

reflection:

*Cast your burden on the Lord, and he will sustain you;
he will never permit the righteous to be moved.*
Psalm 55:22

Daily check-in

date:

today I am thankful for:

1.

2.

3.

my ONE goal today:

today I will find joy in:

reflection:

> But now thus says the Lord, he who created you, O Jacob,
> he who formed you, O Israel:
> "Fear not, for I have redeemed you;
> I have called you by name, you are mine...
> Isaiah 43:1

Daily check-in

date:

today I am thankful for:

1.
2.
3.

my ONE goal today:

today I will find joy in:

reflection:

Therefore do not be ashamed of the testimony about our Lord, nor of me his prisoner, but share in suffering for the gospel by the power of God…
2 Timothy 1:8

Daily check-in

date: _____

today I am thankful for:

1. _____

2. _____

3. _____

my ONE goal today:

_____

today I will find joy in:

_____

reflection:

_____
_____
_____
_____
_____
_____
_____

And after you have suffered a little while, the God of all grace, who has called you to his eternal glory in Christ, will himself restore, confirm, strengthen, and establish you.

1 Peter 5:10

Daily check-in

date:

today I am thankful for:

1.
2.
3.

my ONE goal today:

today I will find joy in:

reflection:

*Be watchful, stand firm in the faith, act like men, be strong.
Let all that you do be done in love.*
1 Corinthians 16:13-14

Daily check-in

date:

today I am thankful for:

1.

2.

3.

my ONE goal today:

today I will find joy in:

reflection:

For I am sure that neither death nor life, nor angels nor rulers, nor things present nor things to come, nor powers, nor height nor depth, nor anything else in all creation, will be able to separate us from the love of God in Christ Jesus our Lord.
Romans 8:38-39

Daily check-in

date: _____

today I am thankful for:

1. _____
2. _____
3. _____

my ONE goal today:

_____

today I will find joy in:

_____

reflection:

_____
_____
_____
_____
_____
_____
_____
_____
_____

*When the righteous cry for help, the Lord hears
and delivers them out of all their troubles.
Psalm 34:17*

Daily check-in

date: _____

today I am thankful for:

1. _____

2. _____

3. _____

my ONE goal today:

_____

today I will find joy in:

_____

reflection:

_____
_____
_____
_____
_____
_____
_____
_____

In all your ways acknowledge him,
and he will make straight your paths.
Proverbs 3:6

Daily check-in

date:

today I am thankful for:

1.
2.
3.

my ONE goal today:

today I will find joy in:

reflection:

*The Lord is on my side; I will not fear.
What can man do to me?*
Psalm 118:6

Daily check-in

date:

today I am thankful for:

1.

2.

3.

my ONE goal today:

today I will find joy in:

reflection:

> I lift up my eyes to the hills.
> From where does my help come?
> My help comes from the Lord,
> who made heaven and earth.
> Psalm 121:1-2

Daily check-in

date: _____

today I am thankful for:

1. _____
2. _____
3. _____

my ONE goal today:

_____

today I will find joy in:

_____

reflection:

_____
_____
_____
_____
_____
_____
_____
_____
_____
_____

Come to me, all who labor and are heavy laden, and I will give you rest.
Matthew 11:28

Daily check-in

date: _____

today I am thankful for:

1. _____

2. _____

3. _____

my ONE goal today:

_____

today I will find joy in:

_____

reflection:

_____
_____
_____
_____
_____
_____
_____
_____

Be strong and courageous.
Do not fear or be in dread of them, for it is the Lord your God who goes with you.
He will not leave you or forsake you.
Deuteronomy 31:6

Daily check-in

date:

today I am thankful for:

1.

2.

3.

my ONE goal today:

today I will find joy in:

reflection:

*Therefore, since we are surrounded by so great a cloud of witnesses,
let us also lay aside every weight, and sin which clings so closely, and
let us run with endurance the race that is set before us...*

Hebrews 12:1

Daily check-in

date:

today I am thankful for:

1.

2.

3.

my ONE goal today:

today I will find joy in:

reflection:

...I am the one who helps you, declares the Lord;
your Redeemer is the Holy One of Israel.
Isaiah 41:14

Daily check-in

date:

today I am thankful for:

1.

2.

3.

my ONE goal today:

today I will find joy in:

reflection:

And the angel answered her, "The Holy Spirit will come upon you, and the power of the Most High will overshadow you; therefore the child to be born will be called holy—the Son of God. And behold, your relative Elizabeth in her old age has also conceived a son, and this is the sixth month with her who was called barren. For nothing will be impossible with God."
Luke 1:35-37

Monthly check-in

How are you feeling right now, in this moment?

| Depressed | Sad | Neutral | Happy | Joyful |

Name 5 dominant emotions this past month:

_____

_____

_____

_____

_____

What do you feel good about?

_____

_____

What are some things that trigger negative emotions?

_____

_____

What is ONE thing you can do to improve your mental health next month?

_____

Do not repay anyone evil for evil.
Be careful to do what is right
in the eyes of everyone.
If it is possible, as far as it depends on you,
live at peace with everyone.
Do not take revenge, my dear friends,
but leave room for God's wrath,
for it is written:
"It is mine to avenge; I will repay,"
says the Lord.

Romans 12:17-19

Daily check-in

date:

today I am thankful for:

1.

2.

3.

my ONE goal today:

today I will find joy in:

reflection:

*And I am sure of this, that he who began a good work in you will bring it to completion at the day of Jesus Christ.
It is right for me to feel this way about you all, because I hold you in my heart, for you are all partakers with me of grace,
both in my imprisonment and in the defense and confirmation of the gospel.
Philippians 1:6-7*

Daily check-in

date:

today I am thankful for:

1.

2.

3.

my ONE goal today:

today I will find joy in:

reflection:

I can do all things through him who strengthens me.
Philippians 4:13

Daily check-in

date:

today I am thankful for:

1.
2.
3.

my ONE goal today:

today I will find joy in:

reflection:

*The fear of man lays a snare,
but whoever trusts in the Lord is safe.
Proverbs 29:25*

Daily check-in

date:

today I am thankful for:

1.
2.
3.

my ONE goal today:

today I will find joy in:

reflection:

> Even though I walk through the valley of the shadow of death,
> I will fear no evil, for you are with me;
> your rod and your staff, they comfort me.
> Psalm 23:4

Daily check-in

date:

today I am thankful for:

1.

2.

3.

my ONE goal today:

today I will find joy in:

reflection:

*...I have said these things to you, that in me you may have peace.
In the world you will have tribulation.
But take heart; I have overcome the world.
John 16:33*

Daily check-in

date: _____

today I am thankful for:

1. _____
2. _____
3. _____

my ONE goal today:

_____

today I will find joy in:

_____

reflection:

_____
_____
_____
_____
_____
_____
_____
_____
_____
_____

The Lord is my light and my salvation; whom shall I fear?
The Lord is the stronghold of my life; of whom shall I be afraid?
Psalm 27:1

Daily check-in

date:

today I am thankful for:

1.

2.

3.

my ONE goal today:

today I will find joy in:

reflection:

*Take my yoke upon you, and learn from me,
for I am gentle and lowly in heart, and you will find rest for your souls.
For my yoke is easy, and my burden is light.
Matthew 11:29-30*

Daily check-in

date: _____

today I am thankful for:

1. _____
2. _____
3. _____

my ONE goal today:

_____

today I will find joy in:

_____

reflection:

_____
_____
_____
_____
_____
_____
_____
_____
_____
_____

*I sought the Lord, and he answered me
and delivered me from all my fears.
Psalm 34:4*

Daily check-in

date: _____

today I am thankful for:

1. _____

2. _____

3. _____

my ONE goal today:

_____

today I will find joy in:

_____

reflection:

_____
_____
_____
_____
_____
_____
_____
_____
_____

But the Lord answered her, "Martha, Martha, you are anxious and troubled about many things, but one thing is necessary. Mary has chosen the good portion, which will not be taken away from her."
Luke 10:41-42

Daily check-in

date: _____

today I am thankful for:

1. _____

2. _____

3. _____

my ONE goal today:

_____

today I will find joy in:

_____

reflection:

_____
_____
_____
_____
_____
_____
_____
_____
_____
_____

*The eyes of the Lord are toward the righteous
and his ears toward their cry.
Psalm 34:15*

Daily check-in

date:

today I am thankful for:

1.

2.

3.

my ONE goal today:

today I will find joy in:

reflection:

*So we can confidently say,
"The Lord is my helper; I will not fear;
what can man do to me?"*
Hebrews 13:6

Daily check-in

date:

today I am thankful for:

1.

2.

3.

my ONE goal today:

today I will find joy in:

reflection:

Refrain from anger, and forsake wrath!
Fret not yourself; it tends only to evil.
Psalm 37:8

Daily check-in

date:

today I am thankful for:

1.

2.

3.

my ONE goal today:

today I will find joy in:

reflection:

...fear not, for I am with you;
be not dismayed, for I am your God;
I will strengthen you, I will help you,
I will uphold you with my righteous right hand.
Isaiah 41:10

Daily check-in

date: _____

today I am thankful for:

1. _____
2. _____
3. _____

my ONE goal today:

_____

today I will find joy in:

_____

reflection:

_____
_____
_____
_____
_____
_____
_____
_____
_____

*I will instruct you and teach you in the way you should go;
I will counsel you with my eye upon you.*
Psalm 32:8

Daily check-in

date:

today I am thankful for:

1.

2.

3.

my ONE goal today:

today I will find joy in:

reflection:

*Settle it therefore in your minds not to meditate beforehand how to answer,
for I will give you a mouth and wisdom,
which none of your adversaries will be able to withstand or contradict.
Luke 21:14-15*

Daily check-in

date:

today I am thankful for:

1.

2.

3.

my ONE goal today:

today I will find joy in:

reflection:

*For the evildoers shall be cut off,
but those who wait for the Lord shall inherit the land.
Psalm 37:9*

Daily check-in

date:

today I am thankful for:

1.

2.

3.

my ONE goal today:

today I will find joy in:

reflection:

Yet it was kind of you to share my trouble.
Philippians 4:14

Daily check-in

date: _____

today I am thankful for:

1. _____
2. _____
3. _____

my ONE goal today:

_____

today I will find joy in:

_____

reflection:

_____
_____
_____
_____
_____
_____
_____
_____

> Be not like a horse or a mule, without understanding,
> which must be curbed with bit and bridle,
> or it will not stay near you.
> Many are the sorrows of the wicked,
> but steadfast love surrounds the one who trusts in the Lord.
> Psalm 32:9-10

Daily check-in

date:

today I am thankful for:

1.

2.

3.

my ONE goal today:

today I will find joy in:

reflection:

> But not a hair of your head will perish.
> By your endurance you will gain your lives.
> Luke 21:18-19

Daily check-in

date:

today I am thankful for:

1.

2.

3.

my ONE goal today:

today I will find joy in:

reflection:

*The Lord is on my side as my helper;
I shall look in triumph on those who hate me.
Psalm 118:7*

Daily check-in

date: _____

today I am thankful for:

1. _____
2. _____
3. _____

my ONE goal today:

_____

today I will find joy in:

_____

reflection:

_____
_____
_____
_____
_____
_____
_____
_____

*The Lord is near to the brokenhearted
and saves the crushed in spirit.
Psalm 34:18*

Daily check-in

date: _____

today I am thankful for:

1. _____
2. _____
3. _____

my ONE goal today:

_____

today I will find joy in:

_____

reflection:

_____
_____
_____
_____
_____
_____
_____

Finally, brothers, whatever is true, whatever is honorable, whatever is just, whatever is pure, whatever is lovely, whatever is commendable, if there is any excellence, if there is anything worthy of praise, think about these things.
Philippians 4:8

Daily check-in

date:

today I am thankful for:

1.

2.

3.

my ONE goal today:

today I will find joy in:

reflection:

> "Blessed is the man who trusts in the Lord, whose trust is the Lord.
> He is like a tree planted by water, that sends out its roots by the stream,
> and does not fear when heat comes, for its leaves remain green,
> and is not anxious in the year of drought, for it does not cease to bear fruit."
> Jeremiah 17:7-8

Daily check-in

date:

today I am thankful for:

1.
2.
3.

my ONE goal today:

today I will find joy in:

reflection:

> When you pass through the waters, I will be with you;
> and through the rivers, they shall not overwhelm you;
> when you walk through fire you shall not be burned,
> and the flame shall not consume you.
> Isaiah 43:2

Daily check-in

date: _____

today I am thankful for:

1. _____

2. _____

3. _____

my ONE goal today:

_____

today I will find joy in:

_____

reflection:

_____
_____
_____
_____
_____
_____
_____

Count it all joy, my brothers, when you meet trials of various kinds, for you know that the testing of your faith produces steadfastness. And let steadfastness have its full effect, that you may be perfect and complete, lacking in nothing.
James 1:2-4

Daily check-in

date:

today I am thankful for:

1.
2.
3.

my ONE goal today:

today I will find joy in:

reflection:

> ...that you have learned and received and heard and seen in me—
> practice these things, and the God of peace will be with you.
> Philippians 4:9

Daily check-in

date: _____

today I am thankful for:

1. _____
2. _____
3. _____

my ONE goal today:

_____

today I will find joy in:

_____

reflection:

_____
_____
_____
_____
_____
_____
_____
_____
_____

The angel of the Lord encamps around those who fear him, and delivers them.
Psalm 34:7

Daily check-in

date: _____

today I am thankful for:

1. _____
2. _____
3. _____

my ONE goal today:

_____

today I will find joy in:

_____

reflection:

_____
_____
_____
_____
_____
_____
_____
_____

*Likewise the Spirit helps us in our weakness.
For we do not know what to pray for as we ought,
but the Spirit himself intercedes for us with groanings too deep for words.
Romans 8:26*

Daily check-in

date:

today I am thankful for:

1.

2.

3.

my ONE goal today:

today I will find joy in:

reflection:

*Humble yourselves, therefore, under the mighty hand of God
so that at the proper time he may exalt you, casting all your anxieties on him,
because he cares for you.*
1 Peter 5:6-7

Daily check-in

date: _____

today I am thankful for:

1. _____
2. _____
3. _____

my ONE goal today:

_____

today I will find joy in:

_____

reflection:

_____
_____
_____
_____
_____
_____
_____

*In God, whose word I praise,
in God I trust; I shall not be afraid.
What can flesh do to me?
Psalm 56:4*

Daily check-in

date:

today I am thankful for:

1.

2.

3.

my ONE goal today:

today I will find joy in:

reflection:

And he who searches hearts knows what is the mind of the Spirit, because the Spirit intercedes for the saints according to the will of God.
Romans 8:27

Monthly check-in

How are you feeling right now, in this moment?

| Depressed | Sad | Neutral | Happy | Joyful |

Name 5 dominant emotions this past month:

_____

_____

_____

_____

_____

What do you feel good about?

_____

_____

_____

What are some things that trigger negative emotions?

_____

_____

_____

What is ONE thing you can do to improve your mental health next month?

_____

The Lord
bless you and keep you;
the Lord make his face shine on you
and be gracious to you;
the Lord turn his face toward you
and give you peace.

Numbers 6:24-26

Daily check-in

date: _____

today I am thankful for:

1. _____

2. _____

3. _____

my ONE goal today:

_____

today I will find joy in:

_____

reflection:

_____
_____
_____
_____
_____
_____
_____
_____

*Be sober-minded; be watchful.
Your adversary the devil prowls around like a roaring lion,
seeking someone to devour.*
1 Peter 5:8

Daily check-in

date:

today I am thankful for:

1.
2.
3.

my ONE goal today:

today I will find joy in:

reflection:

*We know that we are from God, and
the whole world lies in the power of the evil one.*
1 John 5:19

Daily check-in

date:

today I am thankful for:

1.
2.
3.

my ONE goal today:

today I will find joy in:

reflection:

*But even if you should suffer for righteousness' sake, you will be blessed.
Have no fear of them, nor be troubled,*
1 Peter 3:14

Daily check-in

date: _____

today I am thankful for:

1. _____

2. _____

3. _____

my ONE goal today:

_____

today I will find joy in:

_____

reflection:

_____

_____

_____

_____

_____

*So we do not lose heart. Though our outer self is wasting away,
our inner self is being renewed day by day.
For this light momentary affliction is preparing for us an eternal weight of glory
beyond all comparison, as we look not to the things that are seen
but to the things that are unseen.
For the things that are seen are transient,
but the things that are unseen are eternal.*
2 Corinthians 4:16-18

Daily check-in

date: _____

today I am thankful for:

1. _____
2. _____
3. _____

my ONE goal today:

_____

today I will find joy in:

_____

reflection:

_____
_____
_____
_____
_____
_____

Therefore I tell you, do not be anxious about your life, what you will eat or what you will drink, nor about your body, what you will put on. Is not life more than food, and the body more than clothing? Look at the birds of the air: they neither sow nor reap nor gather into barns, and yet your heavenly Father feeds them. Are you not of more value than they? And which of you by being anxious can add a single hour to his span of life?
Matthew 6:25-27

Daily check-in

date:

today I am thankful for:

1.

2.

3.

my ONE goal today:

today I will find joy in:

reflection:

Let not your hearts be troubled. Believe in God; believe also in me.
John 14:1

Daily check-in

date:

today I am thankful for:

1.
2.
3.

my ONE goal today:

today I will find joy in:

reflection:

In my Father's house are many rooms. If it were not so, would I have told you that I go to prepare a place for you? And if I go and prepare a place for you, I will come again and will take you to myself, that where I am you may be also. And you know the way to where I am going."
John 14:2-4

Now may the Lord of peace himself give you peace at all times in every way. The Lord be with you all.

2 Thessalonians 3:16

SPECIAL REQUEST

Pay it forward and help other survivors find this journal!

Have you found this journal to be encouraging in your healing journey? Would you like to help other survivors do the same? I hope you've enjoyed journaling as you are *Finding Shelter in the Storm*.

I would be incredibly thankful if you would leave a brief review or a super quick rating for this book wherever you purchased it - even if it's just a few short sentences.

Thank you!

---

www.TrilliumSage.com

transforming powerless victims of narcissistic abuse into
fearless survivors

References

Brennan, D. (2021, March 25). *Mental Health Benefits of Journaling*. WebMD. Retrieved May 29, 2022, from https://www.webmd.com/mental-health/mental-health-benefits-of-journaling

Morin, A. (2015, April 3). *7 Scientifically Proven Benefits of Gratitude*. Www.Psychologytoday.Com. Retrieved May 29, 2022, from https://www.psychologytoday.com/us/blog/what-mentally-strong-people-dont-do/201504/7-scientifically-proven-benefits-gratitude

Morin, A. (2022, May 17). *60 Things To Be Thankful For In Life*. Lifehack. Retrieved May 29, 2022, from https://www.lifehack.org/articles/communication/60-things-thankful-for-life.html

Shutterfly. (2019, February 27). *100 Things To Be Thankful For in Your Life*. Www.Shutterfly.Com. Retrieved May 29, 2022, from https://www.shutterfly.com/ideas/things-to-be-thankful-for/

Made in the USA
Las Vegas, NV
15 June 2022